CHAIRMAN OF THE JOINT CHIEFS OF STAFF GUIDE

J-7
DISTRIBUTION: A, B, C

CJCS Guide 3501
8 June 2012

THE JOINT TRAINING SYSTEM: A GUIDE FOR SENIOR LEADERS

References:

    a. CJCSN 3500.01 Series, "Chairman's Joint Training Guidance"

    b. CJCSI 3500.01 Series, "Joint Training Policy and Guidance for the Armed Forces of United States"

    c. CJCSI 3500.02 Series, "The Universal Joint Task List (UJTL) Policy and Guidance for the Armed Forces of the United States"

    d. CJCSM 3500.03 Series, "Joint Training Manual for the Armed Forces of United States"

    e. CJCSM 3500.04 Series, "Universal Joint Task Manual"

1. Purpose. This guide provides an overview of the Joint Training System (JTS) and highlights the role of senior leadership in the planning, execution, and assessment of joint training.

2. Cancellation. CJCS Guide 3501, 31 July 2008, is canceled.

3. Applicability. This guide applies to the Combatant Commands, Services, Reserve Components, National Guard Bureau (NGB), combat support agencies (CSAs) (including Defense Intelligence Agency, Defense Information Systems Agency, Defense Logistics Agency, Defense Threat Reduction Agency, National Geospatial-Intelligence Agency, National Security Agency, and Defense Contract Management Agency), Joint Staff, standing joint task forces, and other joint organizations to include state and territory joint force headquarters and joint task forces.

4. <u>Releasability</u>. This guide is approved for public release; distribution is unlimited. DoD components (to include the Combatant Commands), other federal agencies, and the public may obtain copies of this guide through the Internet from the CJCS Directives Home Page--
http://www.dtic.mil/cjcs_directives.

5. <u>Effective Date</u>. This guide is effective immediately.

WILLIAM E. GORTNEY
VADM, USN
Director, Joint Staff

Enclosures:
    A—Introduction
    B—Goals and Vision
    C—Key Reference Documents
    D—Joint Training System
    E—Joint Training Information Management System
    F—Universal Joint Tasks
    G—Joint Lessons Learned Program
    H—Joint Training System Summary
    GL—Glossary

TABLE OF CONTENTS

ENCLOSURE A

INTRODUCTION

> "Our joint force must be shaped as an adaptive, resilient, and agile force that can be employed in the full range of military operations."
>
> **2011 Chairman's Risk Assessment Report**

This guide is designed to help Combatant Commanders (CCDRs), subordinate joint force commanders (JFCs), combat support agency (CSA) directors, functional or Service component commanders, and other senior leaders understand the value and importance of the Joint Training System (JTS). More importantly, it will emphasize their role in using the JTS to develop and manage the training of their organizations to accomplish assigned missions.

1. Background

    a. The Guidance for Employment of the Force (GEF), the Global Force Management Implementation Guidance (GFMIG), the Joint Strategic Capabilities Plan (JSCP), and the Unified Command Plan (UCP) are the principal sources of guidance for Combatant Command (CCMD) steady-state campaign, contingency, and posture planning efforts, which inform subsequent development of supporting joint training programs.

    b. The GEF consolidates Department strategic planning guidance documents to reflect both desired regional/functional security end states as well as contingency planning guidance. The GEF, GFMIG, JSCP, and UCP support the development of theater campaign plans (TCPs) for Geographic Combatant Commands (GCCs) and campaign support plans (CSPs) for Functional Combatant Commands (FCCs), Military Departments, and CSAs. The TCP becomes the mechanism for organizing, integrating, and prioritizing security cooperation activities. The campaign plans "operationalize" CCMD theater or functional strategies by designing, organizing, integrating, and executing security cooperation activities, to include training and exercise events. These activities are designed to promote acceptable international behavior by potential adversaries, sustain peace and security under conditions that promote U.S. national interests, or set the conditions for military success if a contingency cannot be prevented.

c. The GEF and JSCP, through the priorities established by the commander in the TCP/CSP, will provide exercise planners with clear guidance on objectives and priorities. CCMD training programs frequently support both campaign and contingency plan objectives. As a result, exercises should reflect GEF regional or functional priorities.

2. <u>Joint Training System (JTS)</u>. The JTS is a four-phase iterative set of processes that aligns joint training strategy with assigned missions to produce trained and ready individuals, staffs, and units. Although the application of the JTS is deliberate in concept, it is flexible in execution. The JTS assists commanders at all echelons in defining the required level of individual, staff, and collective performance; determining the current level(s) of performance; executing training programs to improve performance; and, finally, assessing those levels of performance relative to mission capability requirements. The capabilities-based JTS set of processes is focused on training requirements identification, planning, event execution, evaluation, and assessment; however, the JTS is also a suitable means for harmonizing joint training with joint force development requirements. The JTS four-phased approach is appropriate for aligning and integrating valid joint concepts and solutions, along with lessons learned and emerging doctrine, into joint training to address joint mission readiness as well as joint force development requirements.

3. <u>Importance of the Joint Training System</u>. The JTS is the command's training system. In broad terms, the JTS is designed to ensure the U.S. Armed Forces are trained and prepared to counter violent extremism, deter and defeat aggression, and strengthen international and regional security. More specifically, it provides a capabilities-based method for aligning training programs with assigned missions (GEF, GFMIG, JSCP, and UCP) consistent with command priorities, capabilities (both current and proposed), and available resources (TCP/CSP). The Joint Training Information Management System (JTIMS) is a Web-based tool suite that, in conjunction with the Defense Readiness Reporting System (DRRS) and the Joint Lessons Learned Information System (JLLIS), provides a set of integrated information management capabilities to identify, collect, analyze, store, and disseminate the data required to support implementation of the JTS and sustain a command joint training program.

4. <u>Tenets of Joint Training</u>. The following six basic tenets of joint training are intended as guiding principles to be applied by commanders and agency directors in developing their joint training plans (JTPs).

a. <u>Use Joint Doctrine</u>. Joint doctrine establishes guidance on how best to employ national military power to achieve strategic ends. It provides the fundamental principles that guide the employment of U.S. military forces in coordinated action toward a common objective. Joint doctrine contained in joint publications also includes a set of common terms, tactics, techniques, and procedures. Joint doctrine provides the basis for joint education and joint training, as well as the planning and execution of joint operations.

b. <u>Commanders and Agency Directors are the Primary Trainers</u>. Commanders and directors at all echelons are responsible for preparing their command to accomplish assigned missions.

c. <u>Mission Focus</u>. Commanders and CSA directors will ensure their training programs are focused on their mission-essential tasks (METs). A successful training program can be achieved when commanders and agency directors consciously focus their training efforts on a prioritized set of training requirements derived from their mission requirements.

d. <u>Train the Way You Intend to Operate</u>. Joint training must be based on realistic conditions and standards. Training shall resemble the conditions of actual operations to the maximum extent possible and use existing operational information networks. Commanders should also feel free to explore recommended alternative ways to accomplish anticipated missions.

e. <u>Centralize Planning and Decentralize Execution</u>. As with military operations, joint training should employ centralized planning and decentralized execution in order to provide operational flexibility while maintaining unity of effort.

f. <u>Link Training Assessment to Readiness Assessment</u>. A military capability is the ability to accomplish essential tasks to standard and comprises one or more of the following elements: doctrine, organization, training, materiel, leadership and education, personnel, facilities, and policy (DOTMLPF-P). Training assessments describe the training element level of the command's training proficiency to accomplish its essential tasks to standard. Commanders and their staff will use joint training assessment data to support their overall readiness assessment in DRRS.

5. <u>Joint Training System in Perspective</u>. Throughout history, military training has evolved with the nature of the strategic environment. The case can be made that U.S. and allied forces fought jointly during WWII and before. However, they did so out of necessity but not necessarily design, in order to bring the greatest amount of force to the enemy in the most efficient manner possible. Training to fight jointly did not come to full

fruition in the U.S. military until the 1990s. Following the Operation DESERT STORM after-action review (AAR), the Chairman and the Joint Chiefs of Staff determined the need to institutionalize a "mission-to-task" (requirements-based) training system aimed at improving joint readiness. CJCS policy and guidance directed the evolution of joint training from events-based training to requirements-based training that is embodied in the four-phase JTS. The JTS was initiated by the Chairman in FY 1994, fully implemented in the CCMDs in 1998, and directed for DoD-wide implementation in 2004. The JTS is now a capabilities-based system, having evolved in consonance with other key DoD systems as national security and national military strategies took on a capabilities-based construct.

6. <u>Commander's/Director's Responsibilities</u>. As a commander or agency director, what are your responsibilities with regard to joint or agency training and where can command or agency emphasis be placed with best results? The following **guidelines** identify those areas where commanders and CSA directors have specific responsibilities. These responsibilities will be stressed throughout this guide to show where the commander or director has specific input as well as overall responsibility. Additional detail and guidance is found in reference b.

    a. Designate staff office of primary responsibility for joint training and ensure the JTS is employed to manage training within the command.

    b. Provide authoritative direction on all aspects of joint training to subordinate commands and forces to include requirements for joint/agency mission-essential task lists (J/AMETLs) and JTP development.

    c. All CCDRs are responsible for annually reviewing the command joint mission-essential task list (JMETL) by 30 September.

    d. All CSA directors are responsible for annually reviewing their agency mission-essential task list (AMETL) by 31 December.

    e. Provide commander's and/or director's training guidance to initiate JTP development and refine, as necessary, throughout the development process.

    f. Approve and publish JTP annually.

    (1) Geographic CCDRs publish and distribute JTPs, including JMETLs, to other CCDRs, subordinate JFCs, Service component commands, CSAs, the Joint Staff, and Services via JTIMS by 15 March.

(2) NGB publishes and distributes JTPs, including JMETLs, to CCDRs, CSAs, and the Joint Staff via JTIMS by 31 March.

(3) Functional CCDRs publish and distribute JTPs, including JMETL, to other CCDRs, subordinate joint force commanders, Service component commands, CSAs, the Joint Staff, and Services via JTIMS by 15 May.

(4) CSAs publish and distribute JTPs, including AMETLs, to CCDRs, Service component commands, other CSAs, and the Joint Staff via JTIMS by 15 July.

g. Consider resources available to meet joint/agency training requirements. Initiate prioritization of resource needs.

h. Evaluate the performance of the training audience in achieving training objectives in every training event. Additionally, evaluate the effectiveness of specific training events conducted under your training plans.

i. Identify, validate, and track observations that apply across the Joint Force for resolution within the Joint Lessons Learned Program (JLLP).

j. Assess the command's ability to meet J/AMETL standards. Monthly, assess the command's proficiency using the results of training events in JTIMS, real-world operations, experimental events, lessons learned in JLLIS, and security cooperation activities, and report mission-essential task readiness in DRRS.

k. Identify and report in DRRS, JLLIS, and JTIMS program and resource shortfalls and the impact these shortfalls have on the command's and/or agency's ability to accomplish its joint/agency training requirements.

l. Provide, as directed, trained and ready forces to another CCMD.

(INTENTIONALLY BLANK)

ENCLOSURE B

GOALS AND VISION

> "Do essential things first. There is not enough time for the commander to do everything. Each commander will have to determine wisely what is essential, and assign responsibilities for accomplishment. He should spend the remaining time on near essentials. This is especially true of training. Non-essentials should not take up time required for essentials."
>
> **General Bruce Clark**
> **Commander, U.S. Army Europe**

No system functions properly without guidance or direction. The JTS was developed for the sole purpose of improving joint readiness; thus, the ultimate and continuing goal that drives the application of the JTS is a U.S. military trained and ready to provide a full spectrum of military capabilities and attributes to prevent conflict and win our Nation's wars.

> "Everyone required to conduct military operations will be trained under realistic conditions and to exacting standards, prior to execution of those operations. Personnel selected for joint assignments will be trained prior to reaching their duty location."
>
> **Joint Training Vision**
> **Chairman's Joint Training Policy and Guidance**

U.S. forces must be prepared for employment across the full spectrum of military operations, conducted in a joint environment with multinational partners and requiring interagency coordination. The desired outcome from application of the JTS in the development and management of joint training programs is to ensure a mission capable force that provides the President with a wider range of military options to deter or defeat aggression or any form of coercion against the United States and its allies, friends, and interests.

The JTS supports CCDRs' mission capability requirements while preserving the ability of the Services and CSAs to train on their core competencies. Joint training supports a range of roles and responsibilities in military, interagency, multinational, and intergovernmental contexts and must be flexible, resource efficient, and operationally effective.

1. Improve Joint Readiness

    a. The JTS is designed to improve the ability of joint forces to perform assigned missions under unified command. Readiness enhancement, from a training perspective, starts by determining what tasks individuals, staffs, and units making up the joint force must successfully complete to accomplish their assigned missions. These tasks are selected from the Universal Joint Task List (UJTL) and tailored to the commander's or director's mission through the identification of task standards and conditions. In joint training parlance, these tasks are defined as METs.

    b. Joint readiness, in turn, is assessed and reported by the CCDRs. DoD components are currently in transition from using various systems to manage and report readiness to DRRS. All DoD components will use DRRS for the selection of tasks from the UJTL to build their JMETL and conduct readiness reporting against this list. Joint readiness is assessed against CCDRs' ability to integrate and synchronize assigned forces to meet mission objectives. Complementary to DRRS is a supporting framework for reporting joint readiness—the Joint Combat Capability Assessment (JCCA). The JCCA provides the Chairman with an assessment of the Department of Defense's readiness to execute the National Military Strategy (NMS).

    c. Joint training should be aligned with strategy. Strategic guidance in the National Security Strategy (NSS), the National Defense Strategy (NDS), the NMS, the JSCP, UCP, GEF, and treaties, etc., provides commanders with very specific strategic direction and the missions they must accomplish. The JTS processes are designed to focus the training of individuals, staffs, and units to the specific joint capabilities required to accomplish those missions.

2. Improve Interoperability

    a. The ability of systems, units, or forces to operate in synergy in the execution of assigned tasks is critical to successful operations. This ability to operate effectively together describes interoperability. From a joint training perspective, interoperability is a Service component responsibility. Interoperability training is based on joint doctrine, or where no joint doctrine exists, on Service or special operations forces (SOF) doctrine to prepare forces or staffs from more than one Service component to respond to operational and tactical requirements deemed necessary by CCDRs to execute their assigned missions. Interoperability training involves forces of two or more Service components (including SOF) with no interaction with a CCDR or subordinate JFC or joint staff. An example of Service-sponsored component interoperability training might include air-to-air refueling between aircraft from different Services. The UJTL is a tool that can be used to effectively aid in improving interoperability, as well as joint training and joint operations. The UJTL incorporates a common language to support communication of mission requirements across the DoD community and beyond. Enclosure F discusses the UJTL in detail.

b. The two categories of training are Service and joint. Within both categories, interagency and multinational training can take place at any time. The Services are responsible for both Service and joint training, and all CCDRs are responsible for the joint training of assigned forces.

3. Unified Action

a. The future of joint training is an integrated and synchronized training effort for supporting the Secretary of Defense and the CCDRs.

b. Joint doctrine defines Unified Action as "the synchronization, coordination, and/or integration of the activities of governmental and nongovernmental entities with military operations to achieve unity of effort."[1] Unified Action thereby includes a wide scope of actions, including the synchronization of activities with other government agencies, intergovernmental organizations (IGOs), and coordination with nongovernmental organizations (NGOs) and the private sector taking place within unified commands, subordinate unified commands, or joint task forces to achieve unity of effort. The importance of effective Unified Action is interwoven throughout strategic and operational level doctrine and related approaches and is an essential element of joint training.

c. Achieving an integrated training effort includes training with, but is not limited to, other federal departments and agencies such as the Department of Homeland Security, Department of State, Department of Justice, Department of Transportation, and international agencies such as the International Red Cross and various United Nations High Commissions. DoD components must communicate, coordinate, cooperate, and collaborate, to the maximum extent practicable, with members of the interagency community, state and local governments, tribal authorities, foreign governments singularly or in alliances or coalitions, international IGOs, NGOs, and private sector companies and individuals as appropriate to

---

[1] Joint Publication 1, page II-2.

enable Unified Action. (Note: Joint Publication 3-08, "Interorganizational Coordination During Joint Operations," offers relevant doctrinal guidance regarding working with these important partners.)

d. These agencies play a critical role in success across the entire range of military operations and therefore should be regularly integrated into joint training. Commanders will find they must spend an appreciable amount of time and energy responding to political and diplomatic considerations. In many instances, the military may not be the primary player and may support other lead agencies. Rules of engagement will be more restrictive, and the commander's entire mindset may be required to shift from offensive strategy and tactics to accommodation and restraint.

e. Under all circumstances, a JFC must be aware that the desired end-state is a cohesive network of CCMDs, Service components, and governmental and nongovernmental agencies that will achieve greater efficiency and increased overall operational readiness through joint and integrated training.

ENCLOSURE C

KEY REFERENCE DOCUMENTS

> "As a global force, our military will never be doing only one thing. It will be responsible for a range of missions and activities across the globe of varying scope, duration, and strategic priority. This will place a premium on flexible and adaptable forces that can respond quickly and effectively to a variety of contingencies and potential adversaries"
>
> **Leon E. Panetta**
> **Secretary of Defense**
> **5 January, 2012**

DoD components use JTS processes to identify mission capability requirements. These capability requirements are expressed as METs. The assessment of current proficiency in these METs serves as the foundation for determining the joint training requirements needed to support the generation and sustainment of required capabilities. The following seven documents provide the written framework for the JTS and associated processes and support the implementation of capabilities-based training across the Department of Defense.

- CJCSN 3500.01, "Chairman's Joint Training Guidance"

- CJCSI 3500.01, "Joint Training Policy and Guidance for the Armed Forces of the United States"

- CJCSM 3500.03, "Joint Training Manual"

- CJCSI 3500.02, "Universal Joint Task List Policy and Guidance for the Armed Forces of the United States"

- CJCSM 3500.04, "Universal Joint Task Manual"

- CJCSI 3150.25, "Joint Lessons Learned Program"

- CJCSM 3150.25, "Joint Lessons Learned Program"

Enclosure C

1. <u>Chairman's Joint Training Guidance</u>. This annual notice provides the Chairman's guidance to joint trainers on areas of strategic interest. The notice includes a list of High Interest Training Issues (HITIs) that normally address broad mission areas or operational capabilities requiring focused attention to achieve desired effects in the joint operational environment. Some HITIs will have very specific supporting guidance on observed areas of concern or interest, while others will be less specific but no less important to address. Commanders/directors should consider Chairman's HITIs for special emphasis in their JTPs. Each command should assess the prescribed Chairman's HITIs in relation to theater conditions as key indicators for joint training requirements.

2. <u>Joint Training Policy and Guidance</u>. This instruction describes CJCS policy for joint training as a means to enhance joint readiness. It institutionalizes a capabilities-based JTS and directs commanders to examine their missions and document their command's warfighting requirements using the task lexicon in the UJTL. The Chairman's Joint Training Policy and Guidance reaffirms the role of the commander as the primary trainer and assessor of readiness, as well as the importance of the Defense agencies in supporting the warfighting mission. It derives from and builds upon the principles laid out in the NSS, NDS, and NMS. Moreover, it emphasizes that U.S. forces may be employed across the full range of military operations, most of which will be conducted in a joint environment with multinational partners and will require interagency coordination.

3. <u>Joint Training Manual</u>. Most systems require a "how-to" manual to help guide the user in application. The JTS is no different, and the publication that meets this need is the Joint Training Manual (JTM). Primarily, this manual describes the overall architecture of the JTS and processes to be used throughout the four JTS phases. Each of these phases is discussed in detail in Enclosure D of this guide.

4. <u>Universal Joint Task List Policy and Guidance</u>. This instruction establishes CJCS policy, guidance, and responsibilities for implementation of the UJTL program. This instruction directs that the Chairman's authoritative system of record for Universal Joint Tasks (UJTs) is the online version of the UJTL Task Development Tool (UTDT) available via the Joint Doctrine Education and Training Electronic Information System (JDEIS). It also establishes the minimum required elements of a UJT.

5. <u>Universal Joint Task Manual</u>. The UJT manual describes the purpose, process, and guidelines of the UJTL. It also includes a standard methodology to develop and maintain UJTs. The manual is meant to be used in combination with the UJTL Policy and Guidance and provides detailed information on how to develop UJTs and how to use them to effectively describe joint capabilities required to execute joint missions. The procedures described in these publications are fundamental to implementation and management of the UJT process.

6. <u>Joint Lessons Learned Program Policy</u>. This instruction provides CJCS policy and guidance to the Joint Staff, CCMDs, Services, CSAs, and organizations participating in the Joint Lessons Learned Program (JLLP). It applies to individuals, staff, and collective joint lessons learned programs, and it affirms the commander's/director's role in the gathering, archiving, reporting, and sharing of lessons learned as related to joint training and readiness.

7. <u>Joint Lessons Learned Program Manual</u>. The JLLP manual describes procedures for executing the JLLP. The manual provides guidance on how to collect observations and identify lessons to support improvements in joint doctrine, organization, training, materiel, leadership and education, personnel, facilities, and policy (DOTMLPF-P) through best practices and lessons learned.

(INTENTIONALLY BLANK)

ENCLOSURE D

JOINT TRAINING SYSTEM

> "The forces, units, and systems of all Services must operate together effectively. This effectiveness is achieved in part through interoperability. This includes the development and use of joint doctrine, the development and use of joint operations plans (OPLANs), and the development and use of joint and/or interoperable communications and information systems. It also includes conducting joint training and exercises."
>
> **Joint Publication 1**
> **"Doctrine for the Armed Forces of the United States"**

The Joint Training System (JTS) incorporates methodologies and processes designed to improve CCMD operational joint readiness by linking joint plans, joint training, and joint readiness assessment to critical mission capability requirements identified as command or agency J/AMETL. The focus of the JTS is primarily on CCMD joint training programs and responsibilities; however, the training management practices and orientation to CCMD capability requirements apply to any CCMD, subordinate joint force command, CSA, or Service component.

As a deliberate set of processes, the JTS is also suitable for integrating valid joint concepts, solutions, lessons learned, and emerging doctrine into joint training to transition new capabilities to the joint operational force.

Any system, no matter how well thought out or well conceived, is of little value unless people are trained and encouraged to use it. Therefore, it is important to assign responsibility for joint training program management across all functional disciplines within your staff. The processes of J/AMETL development, of determining training objectives, and of developing the JTP all require the skill and corporate knowledge of many personnel on your staff. What are the joint training requirements of your staff? What courseware is available to enhance their level of expertise in the JTS? These considerations will help you develop a well-trained staff capable of truly using the JTS. Avoid making one individual the "joint training person." Train the entire staff to use the system and to understand their role in implementing it throughout organization training.

The JTS consists of four phases, beginning with the identification of the organization's required critical mission capabilities based on assigned missions, proceeding through the planning and scheduling of training events, the execution, observation, and evaluation of required training, and finally, an assessment of training proficiency against required capability. The results of the Assessment Phase then feed back into the JTS processes, driving the next iteration of the training cycle. The JTS iterative cycle of processes is shown in Figure D-1.

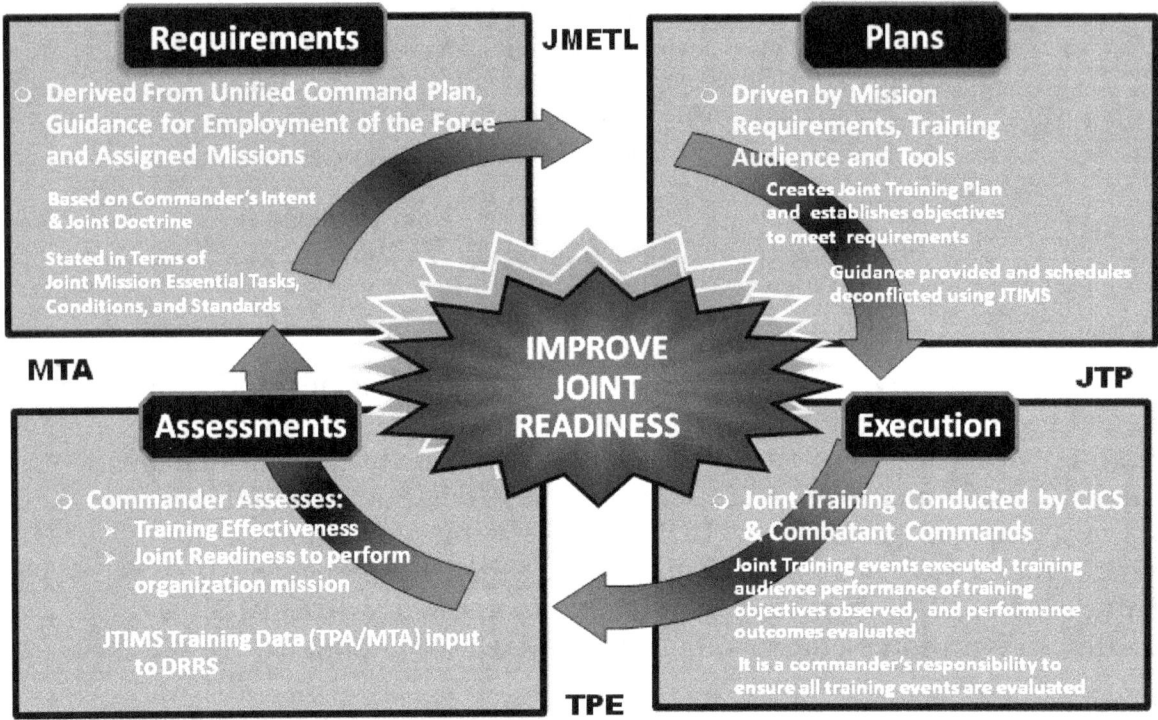

Figure D–1. Joint Training System

1. <u>Phase I—Requirements Phase</u>

a. In this phase, the commander/director answers the question, "What must my organization be able to do?" The purpose here is to define mission capability requirements in terms of tasks that must be performed and the responsible organizations assigned to accomplish those tasks at all levels throughout the force. Sources from which missions, and ultimately tasks, are derived include the NMS, UCP, JSCP, GEF, GFMIG, joint doctrine, and commander's directives.

b. A J/AMETL incorporates those tasks that are essential to a CCMD's/agency's ability to perform assigned missions. The command/agency J/AMETL results from the mission analysis conducted during this phase and provides the supporting documentation from which training requirements are derived. While the development of the command J/AMETL is not an inherent training function, the J/AMETL is fundamental to the joint training processes described and implemented through the joint training system. In most organizations, the J/AMETL development is a command-wide endeavor with all staff elements represented and contributing to a command process led by the J3 and/or J5. Commanders/directors select "best fit" joint mission-essential tasks (JMETs) from the approved UJTL database in the development of their respective J/AMETL and then further tailor tasks for their organization through the application of specific conditions and standards. The command/agency J/AMETL is entered into DRRS through its JMETL development tool and then pushed to JTIMS for use throughout the remaining JTS phases.

c. The UJTL, J/AMETLs from other commands, and joint doctrine assist CCDRs and agency directors in developing their specific METs in the format and language required. A sample JMET is shown in Figure D-2.

JMET: Conduct Information Operations (IO) (ST 5.5) (J3)

UJTL Description: To conduct information operations in support of national military strategy, policy, objectives, and operations.

Responsible Organization: J-3

Condition(s):
C 2.3.2.3   Flexibility of warfare style (flexible)
C 2.4.4   Theater intelligence organization (mature)

Standard(s):
90 percent of subordinate plans have integrated command and control warfare (C2W) efforts
Ten days to achieve information superiority

Supporting Task: Determine Enemy's Operational Capabilities (OP 2.4.1.2)

Responsible Organization: Air Component

Condition(s): C 2.3.2 Military style (predictable)

Standard(s): 10 hours or less required to identify enemy strategic centers of gravity
Command-Linked Task: Support National and JTF Surveillance Reconnaissance Requirements (ST 2.2.2)

Responsible Organization: USSTRATCOM

Condition(s):
 C 1.3.2 Visibility (high)
C 2.7.3.2   Space platforms availability (high)

Standard(s): 90 percent of Joint Operating Area has surveillance coverage

---

Figure D–2. Sample Joint Mission-Essential Task

d. Once the command's JMETs are identified, supporting tasks must also be determined. Staff tasks, subordinate unit tasks, and command-linked tasks are all supporting tasks that contribute to the accomplishment of a JMET. Staff tasks are performed by CCMD staff elements and are their mission-essential staff list. Subordinate unit tasks are performed by subordinate commands and Service components within the CCMD. Command-linked tasks are performed by other supporting CCMDs, CSAs, or other joint organizations not assigned to the supported CCMD. Command-linked tasks depict the interface between supported and supporting commands and contribute to the accomplishment of the supported command's JMET. The Requirements Phase of the JTS (Input/Process/Output) is depicted in Figure D-3.

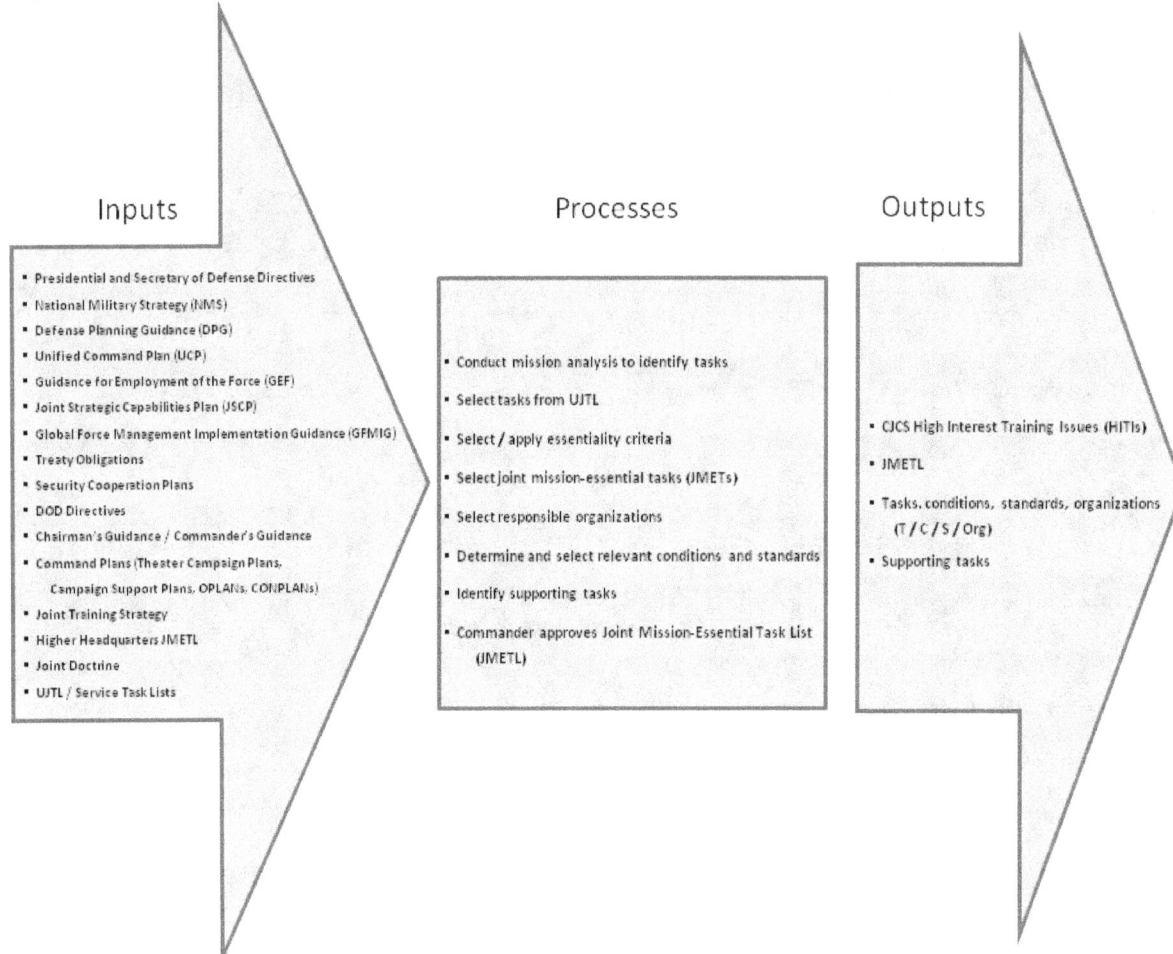

Inputs

- Presidential and Secretary of Defense Directives
- National Military Strategy (NMS)
- Defense Planning Guidance (DPG)
- Unified Command Plan (UCP)
- Guidance for Employment of the Force (GEF)
- Joint Strategic Capabilities Plan (JSCP)
- Global Force Management Implementation Guidance (GFMIG)
- Treaty Obligations
- Security Cooperation Plans
- DOD Directives
- Chairman's Guidance / Commander's Guidance
- Command Plans (Theater Campaign Plans, Campaign Support Plans, OPLANs, CONPLANs)
- Joint Training Strategy
- Higher Headquarters JMETL
- Joint Doctrine
- UJTL / Service Task Lists

Processes

- Conduct mission analysis to identify tasks
- Select tasks from UJTL
- Select / apply essentiality criteria
- Select joint mission-essential tasks (JMETs)
- Select responsible organizations
- Determine and select relevant conditions and standards
- Identify supporting tasks
- Commander approves Joint Mission-Essential Task List (JMETL)

Outputs

- CJCS High Interest Training Issues (HITIs)
- JMETL
- Tasks, conditions, standards, organizations (T / C / S / Org)
- Supporting tasks

Figure D–3. Joint Training System Requirements Phase

2. <u>Phase II—Planning Phase</u>

a. This phase begins once a command/agency J/AMETL is developed and approved. At this point, the commander asks, "What are my current capabilities?", "What training is needed?", "Who must be trained?", "What innovations or alternative capabilities may improve on my current capabilities?", and "What are my priorities?" *In answering these questions, the commander identifies the training requirements, provides essential training guidance to his staff, and initiates the Planning Phase.*

b. Training requirements are identified following an assessment of current capability against required capability, represented in the J/AMETL's training proficiency assessments (TPAs) and mission training assessments (MTAs). Training objectives are then developed to fulfill each training requirement against J/AMETs and staff tasks requiring improvement, implementation, and sustainment.

c. A joint training objective is a statement that describes the desired outcome of a joint training activity for a specific audience in terms of performance, training situation, and level of performance. Training objectives are derived from JMETs, conditions, and standards and based on joint doctrine, commander's guidance, and organizational standing operating procedures. JLLIS provides issues, best practices, or lessons learned data that can support the command's/agencies development or refinement of task training objectives. Training objectives provide the basis for building individual command JTPs that deconflict demand for resources and joint training support across the joint community

d. Related training objectives are grouped into training events, and the appropriate training method, mode, and media are selected based on the level of proficiency of the training audience, desired training outcome, perishability of the training, and resources (time, personnel, funding) available to train.

**Joint Training Plan
Table of Contents**

Commander/Director Training Guidance	Tab A
Mission Capability Matrix	Tab B
Joint/Agency Mission Essential Task List	Tab C
J/AMETL / Training Audience Assessment Matrix	Tab D
Training Objectives	Tab E
Event Summaries	Tab F
Timeline	Tab G
High Interest Training Requirements	Tab H

Figure D–4. Joint Training Plan Format

---

e. All these considerations should be identified in the commander's/ director's JTP. The JTP states missions in general terms, restates the J/AMETL, presents commander's training guidance, specifies training audiences, identifies training objectives, and describes planned training events, required resources for training events, training schedule timeline, and CCDR-sponsored joint and component training requirements. (See Figure D–4.)

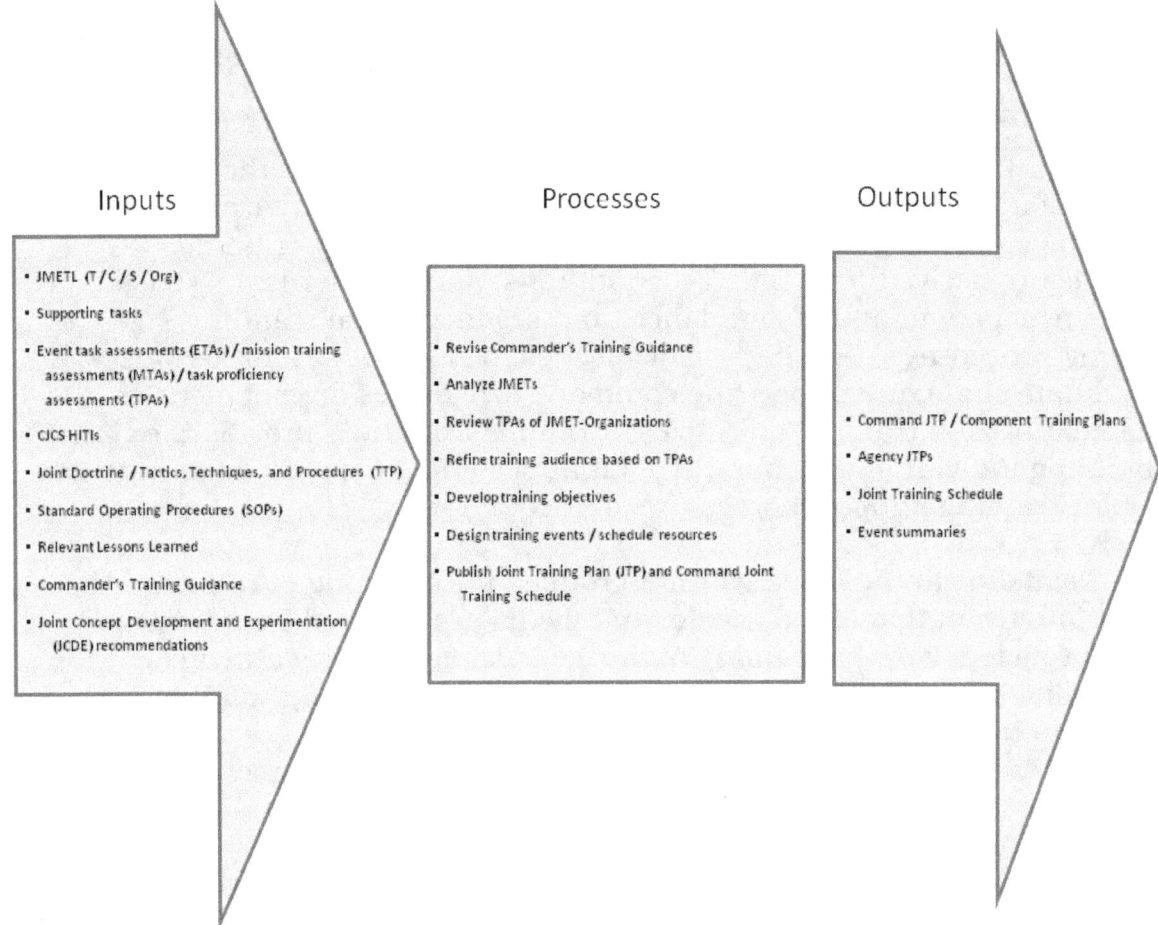

Figure D–5. Joint Training System Plans Phase

f. GCC JTPs are published in JTIMS annually by 15 March so they are available for review by supporting commands and agencies prior to the publishing of their own JTPs (FCC JTPs are published in JTIMS by 15 May, and CSA JTPs are published in JTIMS by 15 July). The NGB JTP is published by 31 March. Figure D-5 depicts the JTS Plans Phase.

3. Phase III—Execution Phase

a. In this phase, commanders and directors focus on executing, observing, and evaluating the planned training events resident in their JTPs. The broad event plans in the JTPs are reiterated in further execution level detail in this phase through a set of processes (stages) collectively defined as the joint event life cycle (JELC) shown in Figure D-6. As stated previously, those training events have been planned to be accomplished through either the academic or exercise methodology or, often, a combination of both methods.

b. Historically, the term "joint training" has been nearly synonymous with "joint exercise." Joint exercises have been generally characterized as some form of multi-echelon, computer-assisted exercise (either field training exercise (FTX) or command post exercise (CPX)) embodying relatively complex simulation and significant support requirements. While joint exercises do represent an important environment in which to conduct specific elements of joint training, there are many more alternatives available to the training planner that should be considered when matching training capability to training requirements and objectives.

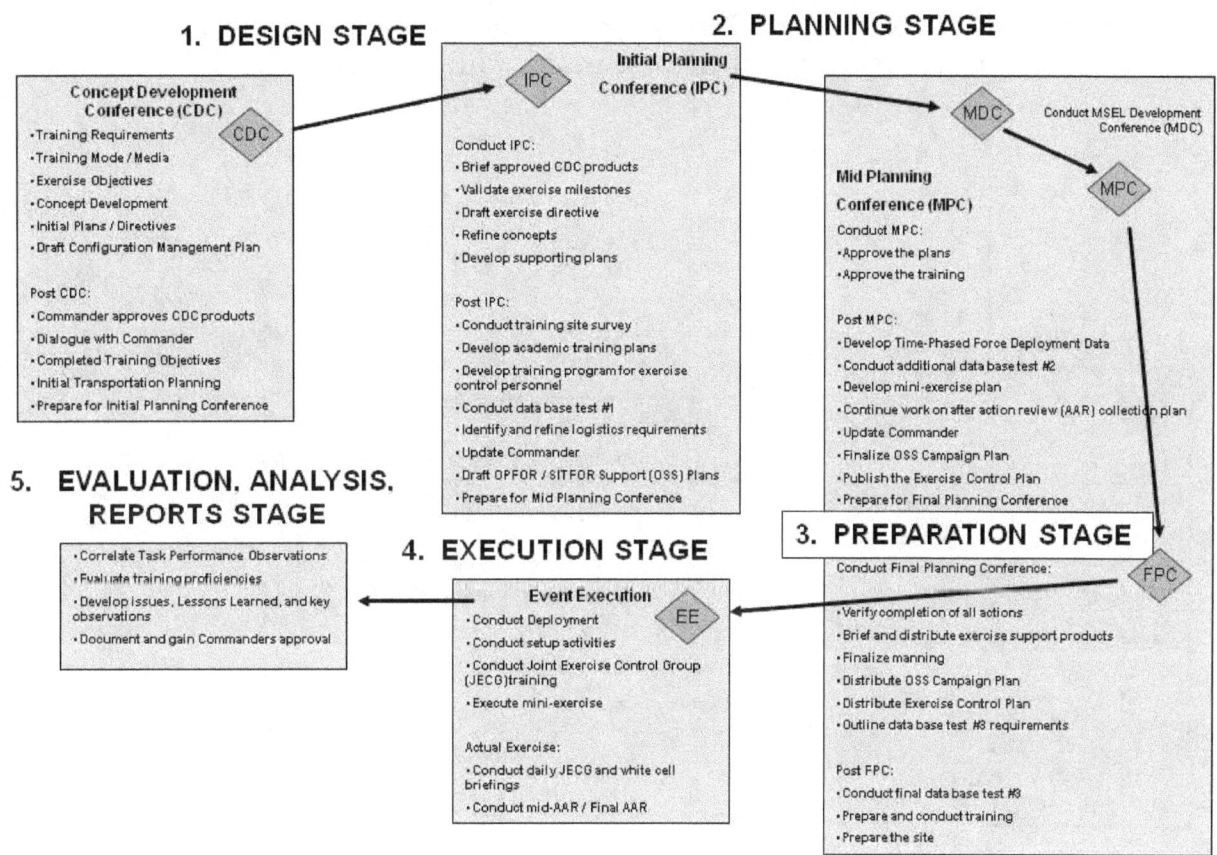

Figure D–6. Joint Event Life Cycle

c. Within the JTS Execution Phase, a JELC is often conducted for each discrete training event. The JELC is a flexible event planning methodology. There are five stages of the JELC, which is often characterized as a "cycle within a cycle." The JELC stages are Design, Planning, Preparation, Execution, and Evaluation, Analysis, and Reports. CJCS policy stipulates that all joint training events will be evaluated. The Evaluation stage of the

JELC is particularly significant because it provides input to guide development of the next training cycle.

d. The length of time to accomplish the JELC for a given training event is dependent on the magnitude and complexity of the event itself. The size and composition of the training audience, training objectives, method and mode of training, selected training media, and other considerations all combine to establish the length of time required to accomplish the JELC for a specific training event. For certain training events using the "academic" method for a small training audience such as a staff element or center, board, or cell, the JELC may be completed in a few days. For training events utilizing the "exercise" method for broader training audiences at multiple echelons such as CCMD, subordinate joint force headquarters, and assigned components, the JELC may span a period of many months, sometimes as much as 18 months for a major joint exercise.

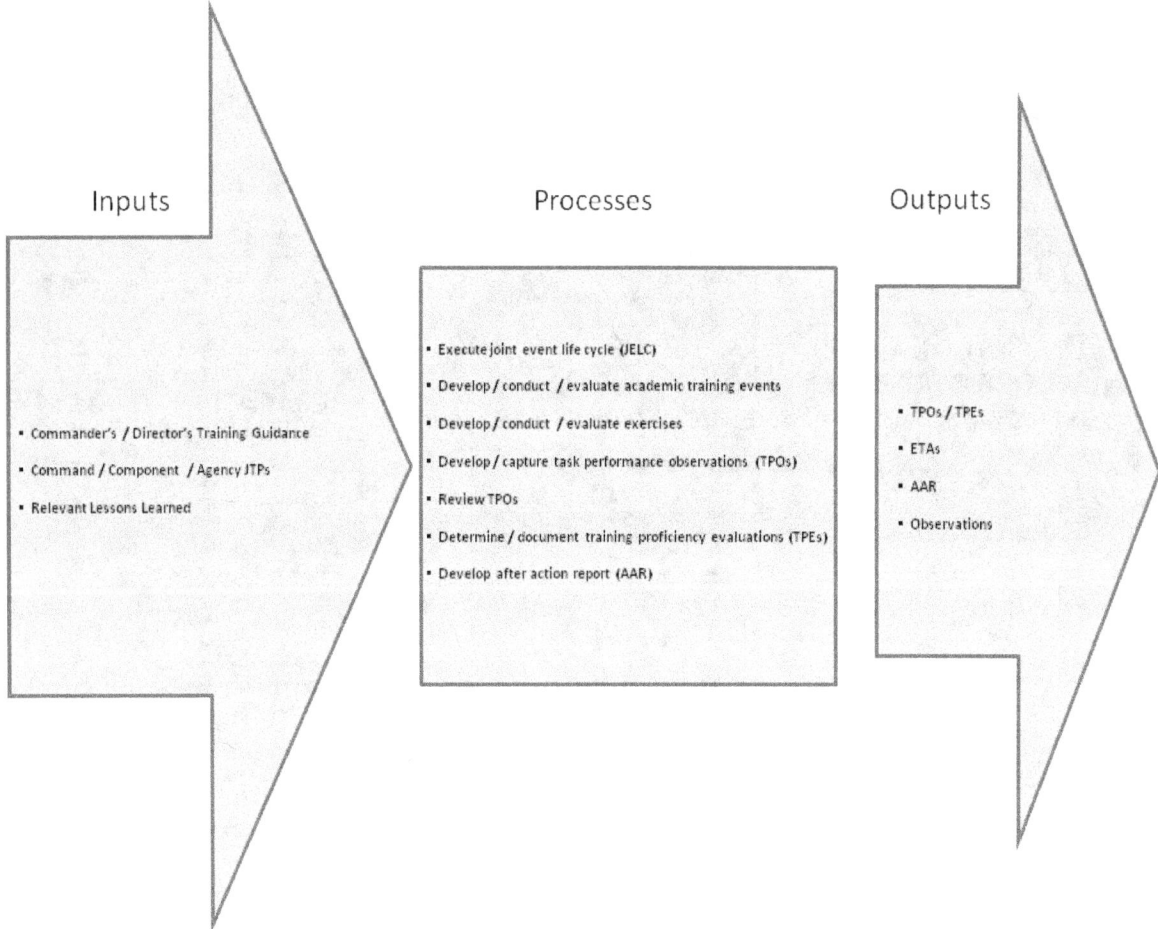

Figure D–7. Joint Training System Execution Phase

e. Evaluation of training is a command responsibility linked to assessments in Phase IV. Designated organizational personnel responsible for training oversight collect task performance observations on whether or not the training audience achieved training objectives and can perform to standard. Training proficiency evaluations also support development of issues for resolution within the JLLP processes. Validated observations from the execution phase are analyzed, validated, and submitted to JLLIS for subsequent action and resolution. These issues, best practices, and observations support future JELCs and the planning/update processes for concept plans and operation plans during the Requirements Phase (Phase I).

f. The outputs of Phase III are task performance observations (TPOs), training proficiency evaluations (TPEs), the Commander's Summary Report (CSR), validated observations for JLLIS, lessons learned, and event task assessments (ETAs), which provide event results that facilitate AARs and highlight potential issues or best practices to support the assessments in Phase IV. The Execution Phase of the JTS is illustrated in Figure D–7.

4. Phase IV—Assessment Phase

a. In this final phase, the commander determines the command's mission capability from the training viewpoint, or, in other words, the command's training assessment (TPAs and MTAs). This assessment contributes to the "training" portion of the command's DRRS readiness reporting responsibilities and is published in real time from JTIMS into DRRS. Although assessments complete the joint training cycle, they also lead into the next cycle, because assessed deficiencies identify follow-on training requirements and inform future training plans. Periodic assessments may also be used to adjust current training plans and training events in the current training cycle.

b. The products from the Execution Phase become the inputs of the Assessment Phase. Actual assessment is performed by the commander, taking into account the results gathered using the assessment plan outlined in the command's JTP. Figure D-8 illustrates the JTS Assessment Phase.

c. The Assessment Phase serves three purposes. First, it provides the structure that allows commanders to view the level of training proficiency in their command against capability requirements identified in Phase I and make judgments on their ability and confidence to accomplish assigned missions. Second, it provides the necessary feedback to adjust or improve training shortfalls and deficiencies (individual, staff, and collective) within the command. Finally, the Assessment Phase supports external processes related to readiness reporting and issue resolution.

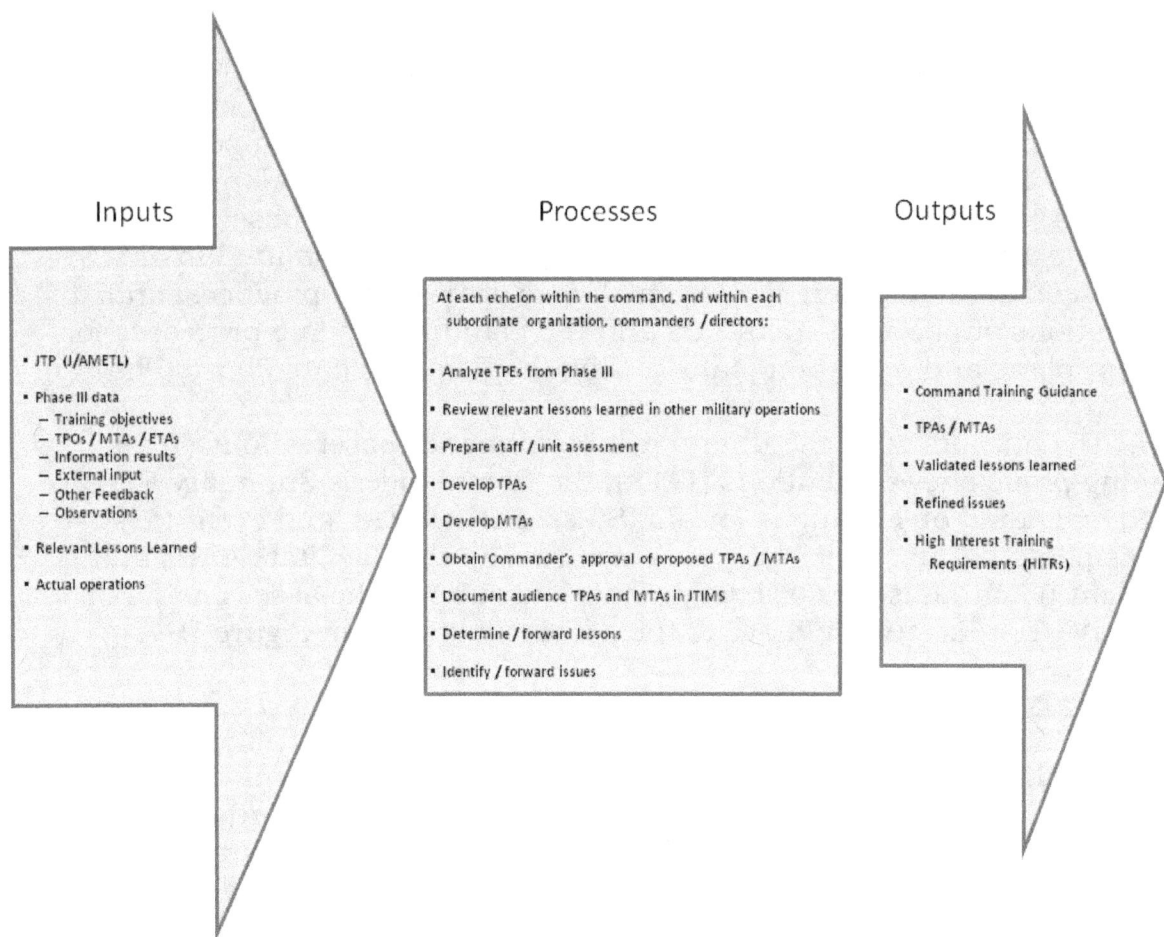

Figure D–8. Joint Training System Assessment Phase

5. <u>Summary</u>. The JTS provides commanders with a set of integrated processes that allow them to look at all of the command's missions and determine which tasks are essential to the successful accomplishment of those missions. The commander can then more effectively focus limited available resources on developing the capability necessary to complete those tasks. Having completed the analysis and prioritization of effort, the commander develops a training plan that identifies who will be trained (training audiences) and the training objectives that will enable the training audiences to achieve the required task proficiency under the specified conditions and to the standards of performance that are required for successful mission accomplishment under the commander's judgment and concept of operations. The commander then executes the plan and follows through with an assessment from a training perspective of the command's ability to accomplish its assigned missions.

ENCLOSURE E

JOINT TRAINING INFORMATION MANAGEMENT SYSTEM

The Joint Training Information Management System (JTIMS) is a Web-based tool that links critical DoD and joint automation programs (i.e., JDEIS, JLLIS, DRRS, and Joint Capabilities Requirements Manager (JCRM)). The functions of JTIMS are as follows:

- Provides integrated information management training support to joint forces and staffs preparing for joint military operations based on joint training capability requirements. The requirements address U.S. military, interagency, and multinational joint individual, staff, and collective organization training.

- Provides support for establishing JTS strategic guidance, goals and objectives, and responsibilities; for planning, executing, and assessing joint training events/milestones.

As previously established, the JTS is a four-phase methodology for aligning training strategy with assigned missions while optimizing the application of resources. These processes are implemented by using JTIMS to provide interactive exchange of information across the JTS phases in support of joint training development, execution, and management.

1. Description. JTIMS is the Chairman's authoritative system of record to support the implementation and execution of the capabilities-based JTS by facilitating the development of an integrated task-based thread to guide application of all four phases of the JTS. JTIMS supports the JTS with information management capabilities as described in the following sections.

2. Phase I—Requirements Phase. JTIMS supports linkage to DRRS. CCDRs, Service component commanders, CSAs, and subordinate JFCs will develop J/AMETLs in DRRS and import them into the JTIMS via Web services.

3. Phase II—Planning Phase. JTIMS supports the preparation of JFCs', supporting commanders', and CSAs' integrated JTPs. It will also support the collaborative development/production of global and local joint training schedules to include an online scheduling and deconfliction capability. Finally, JTIMS supports the initial development of joint training events and supports the JELC as the system of record for requesting capabilities for joint exercises.

4. Phase III—Training Execution Phase. JTIMS supports training event planning, coordination, execution, review, and analysis. It integrates information for events within JELC stages down to the joint task force component and unit level. This will include stand-alone tools to support execution (i.e., the Joint Master Scenario Event List (JMSEL) and Observation Collection Tool).

5. Phase IV—Assessment Phase. JTIMS supports the assessment of joint training and readiness reporting by providing the capability to produce TPAs for individual J/AMETs and MTAs for J/AMETLs associated with CCMD, supporting command, CSA, and National Guard assigned missions. JTIMS will then export TPA information to the DRRS training assessment tab and in support of MTA development.

6. Benefits. JTIMS provides the following benefits.

    a. Information management support for individual and collective training requirements.

    b. The capability to manage information for large-scale multinational, interagency, intergovernmental training events efficiently and effectively.

    c. Collaboration, planning, and interfaces among different user groups.

    d. A development approach that provides a reusable set of software and procedures that can be readily extended to additional JTS products.

ENCLOSURE F

UNIVERSAL JOINT TASKS

1. Universal Joint Task List

a. The UJTL serves as a library of mission tasks in a common language and functions as a foundation for planning, METL development, readiness reporting, joint training, and joint military operations across the range of military operations at strategic national, strategic theater, operational, and tactical levels of command.

b. The UJTL Development Community (UDC) has representation from all CCMDs, Services, and CSAs. Organizational points of contact (OPOCs) are designated from every organization. OPOCs are the points of contact for all UJTL matters to ensure continuity for their organization and throughout the Department of Defense. OPOCs provide task development assistance to their organization and ensure conformance with UJTL guidelines (references c and d); submit organizational candidates/change requests through the UTDT; conduct UJTL education; and synchronize with their organization's METL development efforts. OPOCs also staff UJT candidates/change requests submitted by the joint community to their organization's subject-matter experts and, in turn, submit their respective organizational "vote" and comments in UTDT.

2. Universal Joint Tasks

a. The minimum required elements of a UJT are a task number, task title, task description, measures, and joint doctrinal reference. The authoritative elements of a UJT are a task number, task title, and task description. The task note/background, measures, and joint doctrinal references are non-authoritative.

b. UJTs define current and potential DoD capabilities. The joint commander or agency director responsible for specific mission tasks will articulate his or her unique mission through the application of standards for task accomplishment within a stated set of conditions. Conditions are variables in relation to the prevailing military, civil, and physical environment impacting the execution of the task. The linkage within each UJT to the appropriate doctrine will detail the "ways and means" for task execution (how to accomplish the task). Each Service publishes its own task list to supplement the UJTL and link appropriate Service tasks to corresponding UJTs.

3. Process. Figure F-1 depicts the process by which tasks are developed and then used to support both joint training and readiness reporting. OPOCs submit candidate tasks using the UTDT. Candidate tasks are staffed to the UDC and, when approved, published to the UTDT and made available on JDEIS for use by CCDRs, agency directors, and others to develop their J/AMETL and report their readiness status through DRRS.

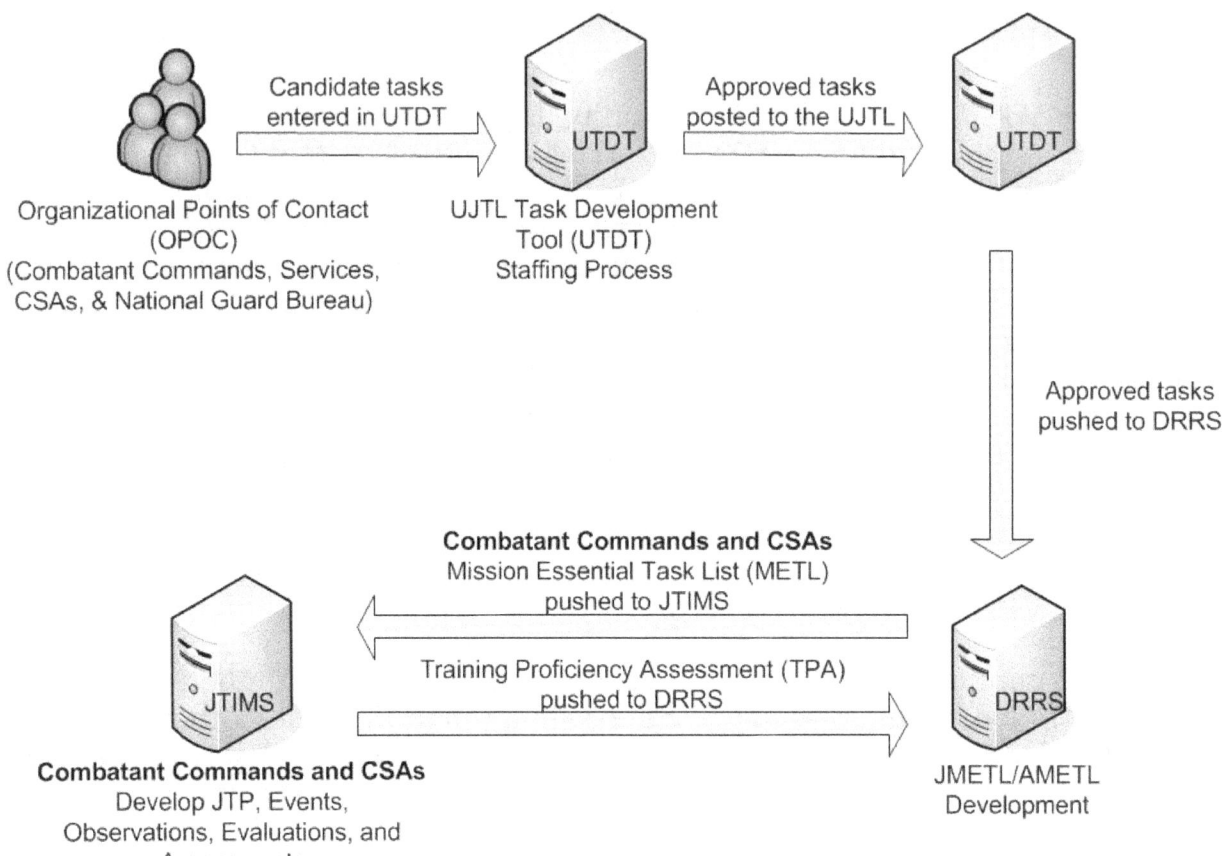

Figure F-1. Life of a Universal Joint Task List Task

ENCLOSURE G

JOINT LESSONS LEARNED PROGRAM

1. Process

a. The Joint Lessons Learned Program (JLLP) provides the joint community with a method to identify, capture, analyze, and share information collected as a result of joint operations, exercises, training events, and other activities for the purpose of enhancing an organization's performance. The Joint Staff J-7 conducts the JLLP in collaboration with the Office of the Secretary of Defense and other interagency organizations. Figure G–1 depicts the JLLP process.

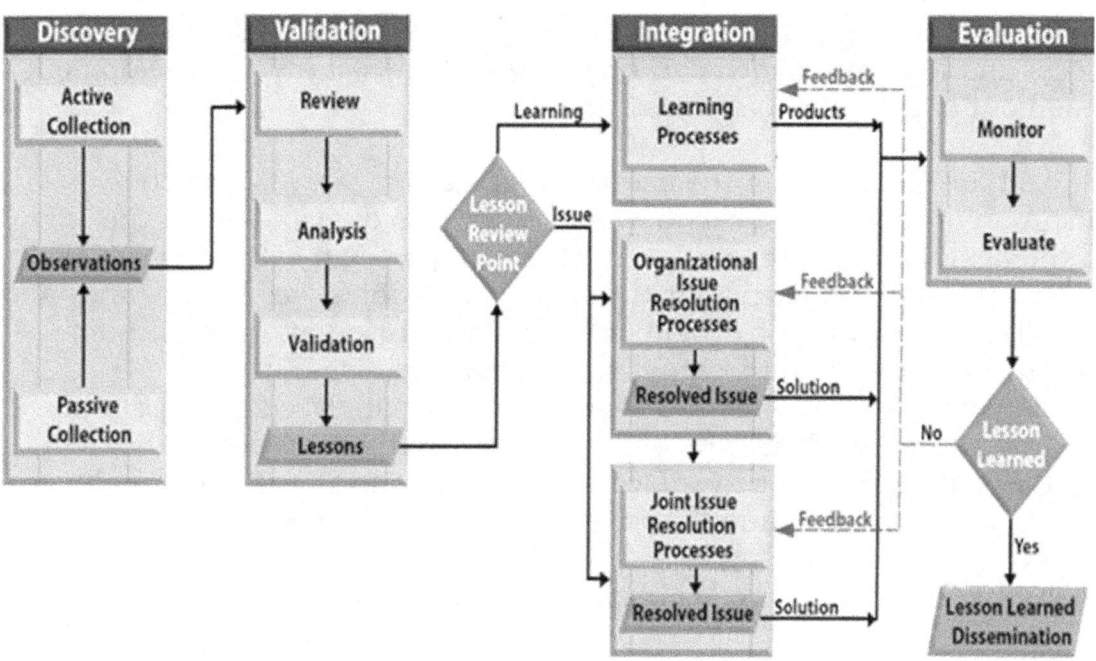

Figure G-1. Joint Lessons Learned Process

b. The CJCS JLLP is a knowledge management activity focused on improving joint preparedness and performance. Its primary objective is to enhance U.S. joint capabilities by contributing to improvements in DOTMLPF-P. It enhances joint force capabilities by enabling learning and collaboration from joint activities including engagement, planning, training, exercises, operations, and joint concept development and experimentation. Current stakeholders are the Joint Staff, Services (to include the Reserve Component), CCMDs, CSAs, and other organizations participating in joint activities. The J-7 assembles strategic lessons learned through direct interviews of key personnel, observations of national level exercises and key events, and the analysis of collected data.

2. <u>Joint Lessons Learned Program and the Joint Training System</u>

a. The JLLP enhances the application of the JTS at several key points during each of the four phases.

(1) Phase I activities are enhanced by surveying the total body of joint lessons learned information. As a command/agency develops its J/AMETL, it leverages the experiences, observations, issues, best practices, and lessons learned discovered by other DoD components. In addition, locally developed findings should also be blended into the requirements development process.

(2) Phase II uses recommendations to improve performance to develop the command training plan. Relevant JLLIS observations, issues, best practices, and lessons learned can be reviewed to assist in the development or refinement of training objectives.

(3) Phase III results in the execution of training events and the identification of validated observations for export to JLLIS. Within the JELC, the design, planning, and preparation steps begin with a review of findings relevant to the particular training event's objectives, tasks, and context. The JTS outlines the deliberate exercise observation validation process to capture key overarching, strategic, and cross-cutting observations and issues. Observations are further analyzed to determine validity and recommended/approved for export to JLLIS. These validated observations, in turn, enter the discovery phases of the JLLP and can be elevated to the issue resolution process. The JLLIS enables commands to selectively share observations across the joint community and elevate validated observations to a formal issue resolution process.

(4) Phase IV activities provide opportunities for the JLLP to both inform the assessment process and benefit from assessment outputs.

b. It is critically important to note that the JLLP does not exist as a support element to the JTS but instead contributes to and benefits from the command's joint training activities. The unconstrained JLLP's visibility into the full range of joint activities, encompassing operations, exercises, experimentation, training, etc., can provide the commander with an invaluable source of relevant information. The JLLP's full inclusion in joint training activities facilitates application of observations and findings derived from training events toward ongoing and future operations and consideration in joint issues resolution and requirements development processes.

3. Joint and Coalition Operational Analysis Division, Joint Staff J-7

a. An important component of the JLLP is the Joint and Coalition Operational Analysis (JCOA) Division, Joint Staff J-7. The JCOA supports transformation of the joint force by producing reports derived from direct observations and analysis of current joint operations, exercises, and experiments that inform the preparation of change recommendations.

b. When requested by the supported command and directed by the Chairman, JCOA conducts active collection during select operations, exercises, and training events; performs functional analysis on the observations; and summarizes findings for joint and national leadership. Recommendations from JCOA's findings are adjudicated across the joint enterprise in accordance with the JLLP's issues resolution process described in the CJCSI 3150.25 series.

c. The JCOA has provided some support to key training events, exercises, wargames, and experiments; however, its highest priority is to provide active collection support during real world operations.

d. JCOA has the ability to work with CCMDs, Services, and interagency and multinational partners for select lessons learned activities, especially those that are particularly important to the Department or that are large in size.

4. Joint Lessons Learned Information System

a. The Joint Lessons Learned Information System (JLLIS) is the Chairman's system of record for the JLLP. JLLIS is the technology support element of the JLLP. JLLIS consists of an input and management support tool and a distributed database. The input and management support tool allows any approved user to submit observations via a Web-enabled user interface. It includes an observation management capability that provides administrative and subject matter expert review, functional classification, and lessons learned release and publishing to the distributed database. JLLIS provides users with a single location to access validated observations, lessons, and issues and has associated search and analytical support tools.

b. JLLIS enables the collection, management, resolution, and dissemination of lessons learned data. JLLIS is designed to facilitate the collection of observations, issues, and best practices from joint activities including engagement, planning, training, exercises, operations, and real world events. Once identified, analyzed and validated, relevant issues, best practices and lessons learned should subsequently influence/inform decisions during the application of JTS Phases I, II, and III processes concerning the analysis, planning, development, resource allocation, generation, and execution of required training that changes behavior and improves performance. JLLIS support to the JLLP phases includes the following.

(1) Phase I—Discovery Phase. Capture observations, issues, summaries and reports.

(2) Phase II—Validation Phase. Analyze observations to produce lessons for the community of practice to conduct learning and issue resolution processes.

(3) Phase III—Integration Phase. Send lessons to appropriate functional organizations for resolution.

(4) Phase IV—Evaluation Phase. Monitor lessons sent to resolution processes, evaluate the learning, and issue solutions to either accept the lessons as lessons learned or return the lesson to the resolution process for further work.

c. Joint Lessons Learned Information System Benefits. The system supports the following lessons learned processes: discovery, validation, integration, and evaluation. It allows dissemination of observations, issues, and lessons learned data across the Department of Defense and participating interagency organizations. It also provides a standard for JLLP data collection and enables issue management. Finally, it provides a robust search capability and a large data repository to support issues resolution and analytical research such as events, operations, and exercise data; observations and recommendations; and AARs.

ENCLOSURE H

JOINT TRAINING SYSTEM SUMMARY

> *"Commanders are the primary trainers."*
>
> **Joint Training Policy, CJCSI 3500.01 Series**
> **"The Six Tenets of Joint Training"**

1. Joint Training System (JTS) Summary. The JTS provides the commander/director with a systematic approach to training. It represents a series of interlocking, logical, and repeatable processes that are intended to continuously improve joint readiness. Used correctly, the system should help CCDRs, subordinate joint force commanders, functional or Service component commanders, other senior commanders, and CSA directors to train more efficiently and effectively while identifying areas for improvement. Effectively utilizing the processes within the JTS better enables commanders to assess the level of readiness in their command and then make informed judgments on their ability to accomplish assigned missions. The JTS set of processes is summarized in Figure H-1 below.

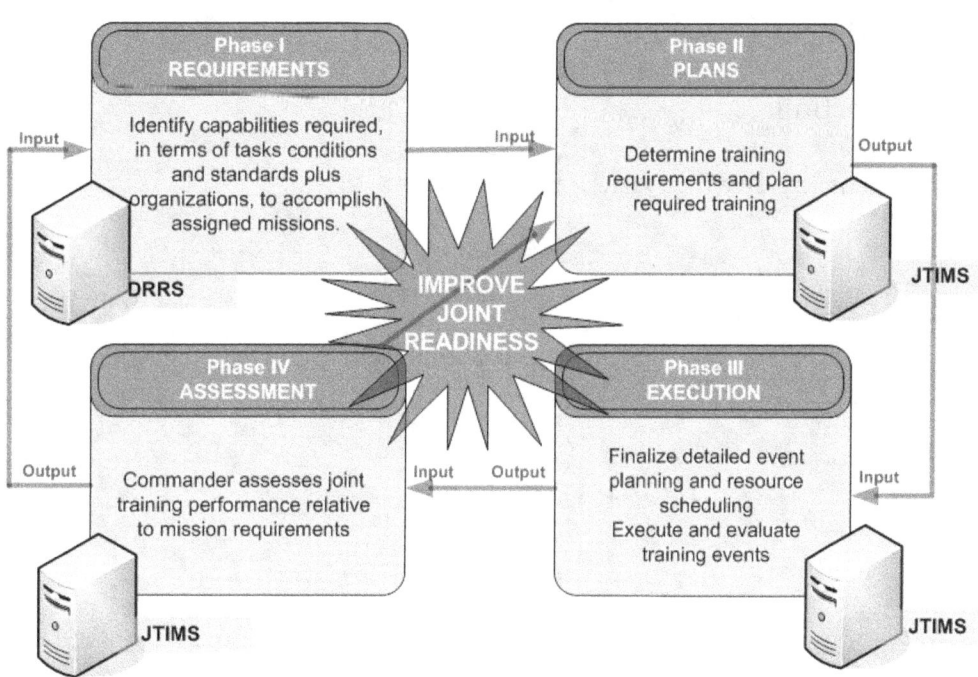

Figure H–1. Joint Training System Process Summary

2. <u>Commander's/Director's Responsibilities</u>. Command interest and emphasis is critical to the success of any training program. Because of the complexity of the joint operational environment, it is imperative that joint training and the JTS remain a priority of all commanders. Enclosure A outlined a commander's/director's responsibilities within the JTS and suggested where command emphasis could best be applied. A summary of those commander/director responsibilities follows:

a. Assign staff responsibilities for joint training.

b. Provide authoritative joint training direction to subordinates.

c. Review and approve annual J/AMETL.

d. Provide training guidance.

e. Approve annual JTP.

f. Effectively and efficiently use resources.

g. Evaluate training audience performance against training objectives.

h. Validate key observations.

i. Assess readiness monthly.

j. Identify shortfalls.

k. Provide/employ trained and ready forces.

GLOSSARY

ABBREVIATIONS AND ACRONYMS

AAR	after-action review
AMETL	agency mission-essential task list
CCDR	Combatant Commander
CCMD	Combatant Command
CPX	command post exercise
CSA	combat support agency
CSP	campaign support plan
CSR	Commander's Summary Report
DOTMLPF-P	doctrine, organization, training, materiel, leadership and education, personnel, facilities, and policy
DRRS	Defense Readiness Reporting System
ETA	event task assessment
FCC	Functional Combatant Command
FTX	field training exercise
GCC	Geographic Combatant Command
GEF	Guidance for Employment of the Force
GFMIG	Global Force Management Implementation Guidance
HITI	high interest training issue
IGO	intergovernmental organization
J/AMETL	joint/agency mission-essential task list
JCCA	Joint Combat Capability Assessment
JCOA	Joint Center for Operational Analysis
JCRM	Joint Capabilities Requirements Manager
JDEIS	Joint Doctrine Education and Training Electronic Information System
JELC	joint event life cycle
JFC	joint force commander
JLLP	Joint Lessons Learned Program
JLLIS	Joint Lessons Learned Information System
JMET	joint mission-essential task
JMETL	joint mission-essential task list
JMSEL	Joint Master Scenario Event List

JSCP	Joint Strategic Capabilities Plan
JTIMS	Joint Training Information Management System
JTM	joint training manual
JTP	joint training plan
JTS	Joint Training System
MET	mission-essential task
METL	mission-essential task list
MTA	mission training assessment
NDS	National Defense Strategy
NGB	National Guard Bureau
NGO	nongovernmental organization
NMS	National Military Strategy
NSS	National Security Strategy
OPOC	organizational point of contact
SOF	special operations forces
TCP	theater campaign plan
TPA	training proficiency assessment
TPE	training proficiency evaluation
TPO	task performance observation
UCP	Unified Command Plan
UDC	UJTL Development Community
UJT	Universal Joint Task
UJTL	Universal Joint Task List
UTDT	Universal Joint Task List Task Development Tool